INTRODUCTION

Your Debt Has Been Paid

Dear Friends,

I love Easter. There's something so special about gathering to worship the risen Savior on Easter morning. It's a time when Christians focus on the sacrifice and glorious resurrection of Jesus, which gives us hope and removes the sting of death.

That is not to say that all of my Easter memories are positive. Several years ago when I was in college, Kendra and I visited my grandparents, Billy and Ruth Graham, for Easter in Montreat, N.C.

On our way back to Liberty University that afternoon, we drove up to Boone, N.C., to see my parents. We pulled into a little gas station on the south side of U.S. Route 70 to fuel up and be on our way.

I stood in line while the people in front of me made friendly conversation with the clerk behind the counter. "Nothing's free anymore," the man chuckled as he handed over the money to pay for his purchase.

At that moment, God told me to speak. My heart was immediately burdened to share the Gospel with these people: "Yes, God's gift of salvation is free! That's what Easter is all about! God paid the debt for you through His Son, Jesus!"

That's what I should have said.

Sadly, I kept that proclamation to myself, and I regret it to this day. The Holy Spirit directed me to speak—and even gave me the words to say—but I disobeyed and remained silent.

I made a covenant with God that day that if I ever felt Him speaking through me again, I would share it boldly. Who knows? Sharing the words He gives us may be the difference between someone spending an eternity in Heaven or in Hell; the difference between a life of hope and a life of discouragement and despair.

As we celebrate Christ's resurrection this year, I hope that you find this devotional to be both a challenge and an encouragement. May this encourage you to listen to God as He speaks to you and be His mouthpiece as He speaks through you.

Blessings,

—Will Graham

"What then shall I do with Jesus?"

PONTIUS PILATE

WEEK ONE

"

Pilate said to them, 'Then what shall I do with Jesus who is called Christ?' They all said, 'Let him be crucified!' And he said, 'Why? What evil has he done?' But they shouted all the more, 'Let him be crucified!' So when Pilate saw that he was gaining nothing, but rather that a riot was beginning, he took water and washed his hands before the crowd, saying, 'I am innocent of this man's blood; see to it yourselves.'

—MATTHEW 27:22-24, ESV

"

EASTER exists because Jesus died for our sins and conquered the grave. We celebrate life at Easter, because death lost its sting with Christ's triumphant resurrection.

Sadly, many have never experienced the true meaning of Easter. They may know of Jesus, but they can't or won't make a decision about Him as their Savior.

In the Bible, we see a man who will forever be linked to what Christ followers call Easter. This man talked to Jesus directly, he evaluated Him, and the Bible says he was greatly impressed with Jesus. Yet he, too, couldn't bring himself to make a decision about what to do with Christ.

His name was Pontius Pilate, and Matthew 27:11–25 tells us a lot about this Roman governor who oversaw the trial of Jesus.

First, Pilate rejected Jesus' own confession of who He was. *"Now Jesus stood before the governor. And the governor asked Him, saying, 'Are You the King of the Jews?' Jesus said to him, 'It is as you say'"* (Matthew 27:11). Pilate asked the question and heard the truth (straight from the mouth of the Son of God), but he took it no further.

Second, Pilate rejected clear evidence. Pilate investigated Jesus and came to the conclusion that He was innocent, finding that He had committed no crime. Pilate realized that the only reason Jesus was on trial was the envy and hatred of the religious leaders, even to the point of appealing to the crowd by asking, "*What evil has He done?*" (Matthew 27:23). He knew the truth but rejected it.

Third, Pilate gave in to pressure. In verse 24, Pilate recognized that "*he was gaining nothing, but rather that a riot was beginning*" (ESV). Though he heard the claims of Christ and knew He had done nothing wrong, Pilate was compelled to sentence an innocent man to death because of the influence of the crowd. He feared man rather than fearing God.

Finally, Pilate tried to cleanse himself from the death of Jesus. He knew that he had just condemned an innocent man to die. In a symbolic gesture, Pilate "*washed his hands before the crowd, saying, 'I am innocent of this man's blood; see to it yourselves'*" (Matthew 27:24, ESV). Understanding and pronouncing that Jesus was blameless, he proclaimed the guilt for Christ's death onto the crowd instead.

My friends, Pilate had a decision to make. He knew the truth, but he couldn't take a stand one way or the other. Instead, he asked a question: *"What then shall I do with Jesus who is called Christ"* (Matthew 27:22)?

That's the question that so many today, perhaps even you, have a hard time answering. In far too many situations, people know the truth, but—like Pilate—they give in to the pressures of others and walk away from Jesus, putting the decision off for another day.

However, indecision is a decision. Making no decision for Christ is making a decision about Christ. By not surrendering your life to Him, you're rejecting the claims of Jesus, that He is the Son of God who died in your place.

If you have been putting off the decision to follow Christ and make Him the Lord of your life, now is the perfect time. Jesus' death and resurrection, which we celebrate as Easter, paved the way for you. I encourage you to receive that hope and accept Him as your Savior today!

Think about a time when you or a friend knew the right decision to make but were swayed by peer pressure. How could the outcome have been different if the correct decision had been made first?

_____

_____

Have you ever let others influence you to turn away from your faith? How or why? What can be done in the future to safeguard against that?

_____

_____

PRAYER:

Lord Jesus, thank You for the sacrifice You made on the cross. No matter what the world says, help me to follow You with all that I have. Help me to live boldly for You every day. In Your Name I pray, amen.

Jesus Paid the Price

BARABBAS

WEEK TWO

Now at the feast the governor was
accustomed to releasing to the multitude
one prisoner whom they wished. And at
that time they had a notorious prisoner
called Barabbas. Therefore, when they had
gathered together, Pilate said to them,
'Whom do you want me to release to you?
Barabbas, or Jesus who is called Christ?'
For he knew that they had handed Him over
because of envy. ... But the chief priests and
elders persuaded the multitudes that they
should ask for Barabbas and destroy Jesus.
The governor answered and said to them,
'Which of the two do you want me to
release to you?' They said, 'Barabbas!'

—MATTHEW 27:15-18, 20-21

J ESUS stood on trial, facing not just the Roman governor Pontius Pilate but also an incited mob intending to "*destroy*" Him (Matthew 27:20). Meanwhile, somewhere in the bowels of the prison, a man named Barabbas sat and awaited his own execution at the hands of the government.

Of the 31,000+ verses in the Bible, Barabbas is the subject of very few. There aren't many details about him historically. However, he's an incredibly consequential character in the history of Christ's sacrifice on the cross.

As the trial was coming to a close, having heard the arguments and having personally questioned Jesus, Pontius Pilate recognized this was an unjust situation. Pilate wanted Jesus to go free, but he was more concerned about appeasing the crowd. Call it a loophole, perhaps, but Pilate gave the crowd a way out of spilling innocent blood. According to custom, Pilate could release one prisoner.

You could say he stacked the deck in Jesus' favor. Next to Jesus, he brought up what was likely the worst death row inmate on his roster. "*Whom do you want me to release to you? Barabbas, or Jesus who is called Christ*" (Matthew 27:17)?

It was a matter of innocence versus evil, yet—to Pilate's surprise—the crowd cried out for the blood of Jesus. Christ was sentenced to death. Barabbas went free.

What do we know about Barabbas?

First, we know Barabbas was a violent insurrectionist. In Mark 15:7, we read that Barabbas *was chained with his fellow rebels; they had committed murder in the rebellion.* That is echoed in Luke 23:25, which says Barabbas was guilty of rebellion and murder. John 18:40 adds robbery to Barabbas' rap sheet.

Second, Barabbas was well known. While for us, Barabbas may seem like a bit player in the Gospels, Matthew 27:16 tells us he was a "*notorious prisoner.*" His violence would have been major news, even in a relatively large city like Jerusalem. When the "*chief priests and elders persuaded the multitudes that they should ask for Barabbas*" (Matthew 27:20), they knew exactly what they were getting in the exchange.

Finally, we know this was a major development in the trial of Christ. While many skeptics have questioned Barabbas' existence, the fact that this transaction is recorded in all four books confirms this event not only happened, but was likely a key and unanticipated turn of events.

There were three crosses on Golgotha (the hill on which Jesus died). Two were reserved for thieves, and the other was intended for Barabbas. It was where he would suffer the consequences and pay for his lawlessness.

But then, unexpectedly, a man he'd never met took his place. Though his punishment was death, he had an opportunity to be free. I don't for a second imagine that he waited or argued. He ran, as far and as fast as he could, to get away from certain death.

On a spiritual level, we're like Barabbas. We're sinners who have fallen short of God's glory (Romans 3:23) and the penalty of that sin is eternal death (Romans 6:23). Jesus has paid the penalty and taken our place, giving us the opportunity for the gift of God, which is eternal life (Romans 6:23).

My friends, Barabbas was smarter than many people today. Jesus took Barabbas' place in going to the cross, and Barabbas didn't hesitate to accept that substitution. Will you accept Christ's death as substitution for eternal death and live with Him in Heaven someday?

Put yourself in Barabbas' place. What emotions would you have felt in that prison cell, awaiting certain execution? How would you have reacted after realizing that someone else was taking your place on the cross, and you were being set free?

_____

_____

If you are a follower of Jesus Christ, describe the freedom you have found in Him. How is your life different now than before you knew Him as Savior?

_____

_____

PRAYER:

Dear Jesus, thank You for taking my place on the cross and paying the debt of my sin. Thank You for the freedom that I now have in You. In Jesus' Name, amen.

The Agony of Betrayal

JUDAS & PETER

"

And the servant girl saw him again, and began to say to those who stood by, 'This is one of them.' But he denied it again. And a little later those who stood by said to Peter again, 'Surely you are one of them; for you are a Galilean, and your speech shows it.' Then he began to curse and swear, 'I do not know this Man of whom you speak!' A second time the rooster crowed. Then Peter called to mind the word that Jesus had said to him, 'Before the rooster crows twice, you will deny Me three times.' And when he thought about it, he wept.

—MARK 14:69–72

"

AS WE THINK about the sacrifice of Jesus, we often focus on the unbearable physical pain He endured. He was hit, flogged, and had a crown of thorns driven into His scalp. He was made to carry His own cross. Nails were punched through His flesh before He was hoisted into the air to suffocate in one of the cruelest forms of punishment ever devised.

It's hard to not focus on the pain He endured for us. But I want you to consider another way Jesus suffered before His crucifixion. Consider the emotional pain Christ endured as those who were closest to Him turned their backs.

Of course, there was the moment when Jesus cried out, "*Eli, Eli, lama sabachthani?*" which means, "*My God, My God, why have You forsaken Me?*" (Matthew 27:46) as God the Father turned His face from His Son, which must have been the most crushing blow of all.

However, let's look at the human element, Christ's "inner circle."

Jesus personally chose 12 disciples whom He poured Himself into. These men could almost be considered His earthly family, spending time with Him, learning from Him, and serving in His ministry. Jesus loved them, and yet He knew—long before they did, in fact—that a couple of these men would publicly betray Him.

Judas, certainly, is the one that often comes to mind. After all, it was his betrayal that led to Jesus' arrest. We're told in Luke 22:3 that "*Satan entered Judas.*" John 13:2 says that the devil put it into Judas' heart to betray Jesus. Judas went to the chief priests and officers, accepted a payment from them, and then actively plotted to betray Jesus into their hands when there wouldn't be a crowd around Him.

Judas' treachery was the ultimate betrayal, directly resulting in a sham trial and the agony of the cross. But I wonder if the second betrayal might not have hurt just as much as the first.

Along with James and John, Peter was one of Jesus' closest friends, whom He chose to be a witness to key moments in His earthly ministry. For instance, Peter was there for Jesus' transfiguration on the mountain and at Gethsemane on the eve of Christ's sacrifice. He even drew a sword and tried to physically defend Jesus as He was being arrested (John 18:10).

Peter's denial of Jesus—which Jesus foretold prior to leaving for Gethsemane—must have stung deeply. As Jesus was being beaten and ridiculed (Mark 14:65), Peter was busy distancing himself from Christ (Mark 14:66–72). Three times people approached Peter to ask him if he was associated with Jesus, and three times

Peter denied Him. *"Then he began to curse and swear, 'I do not know this Man of whom you speak'"* (Mark 14:71)!

In the midst of Christ's anguish, His friends turned their backs on Him. What emotional pain this must have caused, even as Jesus knew it was coming and understood that it had to be!

Maybe you have friends or family members who have turned their backs on you, or perhaps—like Judas—they were instrumental in causing the suffering you are now enduring. Maybe you're struggling, and the people you thought you could depend on have disappeared. Bodily pain hurts physically, but emotional pain slices directly to your soul.

My friends, people will let you down. They will turn their backs on you and cause you pain. But here's the key—Jesus was forsaken, betrayed, and crucified, but He conquered all of that! People are imperfect, but Christ is risen and victorious!

The Bible tells us not to put our faith in men. Instead, this Easter place your eternity in the One who endured pain and betrayal from His friends—including Peter, whom He later restored—and you will have a hope that extends far beyond the suffering of this world.

DISCUSSION QUESTIONS:

How have you reacted when betrayed by friends or family? Likewise, have you hurt a loved one in such a way that you should seek their forgiveness?

_____

_____

What lessons can we learn from Christ's suffering and the betrayals that He endured?

_____

_____

PRAYER:

Lord Jesus, even as You faced the pain of betrayal at the hands of Your dearest friends, I realize that it was my sin that You bore on the cross. You went through all of this for me. Help me to forgive those who have hurt me, and—in turn—give me the humility to ask for forgiveness from those I have hurt. In Jesus' Name, amen.

"Lord, remember me."

THE CRIMINAL ON THE CROSS

WEEK FOUR

"

Then one of the criminals who were hanged blasphemed Him, saying, 'If You are the Christ, save Yourself and us.' But the other, answering, rebuked him, saying, 'Do you not even fear God, seeing you are under the same condemnation? And we indeed justly, for we receive the due reward of our deeds; but this Man has done nothing wrong.' Then he said to Jesus, 'Lord, remember me when You come into Your kingdom.' And Jesus said to him, 'Assuredly, I say to you, today you will be with Me in Paradise.'

—LUKE 23:39-43

"

THE CROSS means different things to different people. For some, it's merely a pretty piece of jewelry. To others, it's a decoration for their home. To Christians, it's a symbol of the sacrificial love of Christ and His conquering of the grave.

To criminals under Roman rule in the first century, however—and to those who witnessed the punishment—the cross was a symbol of torture, incomprehensible suffering, cruelty, death, and humiliation.

As we know, Jesus was not alone when His cross was lifted and dropped into place. *"Then two robbers were crucified with Him, one on the right and another on the left"* (Matthew 27:38).

Imagine the situation: Jesus was the epitome of innocence. He had never sinned (2 Corinthians 5:21), and yet He was arrested, wrongfully convicted, beaten, and hung on the cross. And now, as if that wasn't enough, He was positioned between two thieves who—despite their similar predicaments—mocked Him as well (Matthew 27:44).

Something changed, however. As the three were nailed to their respective crosses, one of the criminals told the other to stop mocking Jesus. As he hung dying, it seems that he had realized a few things. They're lessons we can learn as well.

First, the criminal had a correct view of reality, of himself, and of Jesus. Speaking of their condemnation and execution, the one thief told the other, "*And we indeed justly, for we receive the due reward of our deeds; but this Man has done nothing wrong.*" (Luke 23:41). He saw himself as a criminal who was rightly condemned. He knew he was a sinner, and Jesus was innocent.

The second lesson we learn is that this criminal had a correct view of life after death. In the midst of being executed, clinging to life, he believed that his soul would continue to live after he died. Many people today live as if this life is all there is and that physical death is the end. The Bible, however, says that your soul lives forever and that it will abide in one of two places— Heaven or Hell (Matthew 10:28, Luke 12:5, John 3:1–21).

Finally, we see that this criminal had a correct view of salvation. He saw himself as totally helpless. He could do nothing to improve his odds in life or save himself. He was now bound to death and could not escape. Yet he cries out to Jesus, "*Lord, remember me when You come into Your kingdom*" (Luke 23:42). He wanted to offer the last thing he had to give (his soul) to Jesus. He realized that Jesus was the Son of God and that he wanted to be a part of Christ's kingdom.

The criminal on the cross knew who he was and who Jesus was, he knew that his soul would continue after he died, and he knew that Jesus was the Savior. He could do nothing but cry out to Jesus and place his faith in Him for his salvation. And to this Jesus replied, *"Today you will be with Me in Paradise"* (Luke 23:43).

Have you seen the world through the eyes of this condemned criminal? Do you understand your need for the Savior, and—more importantly—have you cried out to Him for forgiveness, for your salvation?

If not, now is the time to surrender your life to Christ. If you have made that decision, I encourage you to not miss the opportunities God puts in front of you to share that same hope with those around you. Jesus saved the criminal on the cross, and He desires to save each of us as well.

In your opinion, why did the criminal on the cross change his mind and cry out to Jesus?

_____

_____

The criminal could do nothing to change his circumstances—he couldn't go to church, ask for forgiveness from those he had hurt, or serve in his community—and yet Jesus said he would soon see Paradise. What does that tell you about Jesus and salvation?

_____

_____

PRAYER:

Dear Jesus, I'm not that different from the criminal on the cross. I, too, have sinned and have been condemned, but I have found the promise of eternity as I call on Your name. The wages of sin is death, but the gift of God is eternal life. Thank You for the hope I have in You. In Your Name I pray, amen.

Will You Accept His Gift?

HE IS RISEN

WEEK FIVE

THIS DAY, Easter Sunday, is important for one reason. It's not about candy, bunnies, or having a delicious meal with your family. Those things aren't bad, and if you're enjoying them today, I hope you have a blessed time.

The reason today matters is because of Christ's resurrection from the tomb.

As we've detailed over the past few weeks, Jesus was betrayed, put on trial, wrongfully convicted, mocked, beaten, and executed in the cruelest of fashions.

He died, paying the debt for our sins, and was placed in a tomb. 1 John 2:2 says, *"And He Himself is the propitiation [atoning sacrifice] for our sins, and not for ours only but also for the whole world."* 2 Corinthians 5:21 says, *"For He made Him who knew no sin to be sin for us, that we might become the righteousness of God in Him."*

Three days later, in the most pivotal event in human history, Christ rose again! The grave could not hold Him. He conquered death once and for all.

"'O Death, where is your sting? O Hades, where is your victory?' The sting of death is sin, and the strength of sin is the law.

But thanks be to God, who gives us the victory through our Lord Jesus Christ" (1 Corinthians 15:55–57).

The cross represents a new beginning, a fresh hope. Though the Bible says that sin separates us from God (Romans 3:23), we've been given the gift of eternal life in Christ (Romans 6:23). As we call upon His name for salvation, He takes all of our sin, shame, guilt, and sorrow, and gives us a new life in Him.

If you have placed your faith in Jesus as your Savior—if you've repented of your sin, sought His forgiveness, and made Him the Lord of your life—there is no longer any sting in death. There is no more guilt in sin. You have been washed clean. Like the thief on the cross, you will one day be with Jesus in Paradise.

My friends, Jesus died but rose from the grave. As you read this, you may be spiritually dead, but you can be made alive today. You just need to accept the gift of salvation that Jesus offers through His sacrifice and resurrection. It's Easter morning. There's never been a better time.

If you would like to follow Jesus, here's a prayer that you can use to help express your feelings:

"

Dear God, I know I'm a sinner,
and I ask for Your forgiveness.
I believe Jesus Christ is Your
Son. I believe that He died for
my sin and that You raised
Him to life. I want to trust
Him as my Savior and follow
Him as Lord, from this day
forward. Guide my life and
help me to do your will. I pray
this in the Name of Jesus.

AMEN

"

If you prayed that prayer and chose to follow Jesus, you are now a child of God! Please visit **PeaceWithGod.net** to learn more and to let us know about your decision. We'd love to help you grow in your faith.

Wherever you are, thank you for spending the last several weeks with me through this devotional. I pray that you will have a blessed Easter with your family and friends. Praise God for His infinite mercy and profound grace.